BUSINESSLIKE GOVERNMENT

LESSONS LEARNED FROM AMERICA'S BEST COMPANIES

Vice President Al Gore

DILBERT™ comic strips by Scott Adams

NATIONAL PERFORMANCE REVIEW   OCTOBER 1997

TABLE OF CONTENTS

INTRODUCTION

I   **Incorporating Change** 1
Better government is coming to your neighborhood—soon

KEY PRINCIPLES

II   **Taxpayers are Customers Too** 7
Business teaches government about customer service

III   **Creative License** 25
Unleashing the creative power of government employees

ACHIEVEMENTS

IV   **Cutting Waste and Red Tape** 45
Making taxpayers' money go further

V   **Scream Savers** 61
Technology is saving taxpayers time and money

VI   **Do the Right Thing** 79
Regulators are more effective in partnership with industry

THE FUTURE

VII   **Show Me the Reinvention!** 101
Believe that government has been reinvented when you see it

Acknowledgments 107

Index 109

CHAPTER 1

Incorporating Change

Better government is coming to your neighborhood — soon

Fifteen years ago the wheels were falling off the American auto industry. People were buying more and more Japanese cars and fewer and fewer American cars. The Japanese cars were better and cheaper, after all. And the gap was widening.

If somebody had said in 1982 that within 10 years the American auto industry would be producing excellent cars at competitive prices, they would have been met with jeers.

But it happened.

If somebody had said in 1993 that within 10 years the federal government would be smaller, customer-driven, worker-friendly, and run like America's best businesses, they would have drawn worse jeers.

But that was the challenge that President Clinton handed down four years ago when he asked me to reinvent the federal government — to put the wheels back on. We agreed right then that we needed to bring a revolution to the federal government: We call it reinventing government.

So I did two things. I assembled a team of experts — 200-plus federal employees who knew what was wrong and wanted to make it right. And I went to business leaders who had reinvented corporate America, and who were willing to share their insights and experience with government.

Together, we went to work to create a government that works so much better and costs so much less that Americans will regain faith in the institution of government. The stakes in this revolution are high: confidence in our ability to resolve serious national issues like crime, education, and the environment by working together through government. Without that confidence, we abandon the future to chaos.

Over the past four years, I have issued annual reports on our progress. In all these reports, I have told you that the energy and creativity behind government reinvention has come from federal employees themselves. No one knows better what is wrong with government, and no one wants more to fix it. All that remains true. But we have not simply been improvising as we go along, dreaming it up by ourselves.

> *I called on the experts: federal employees and business leaders.*

> **Business told us to focus on our customers, and listen to our workers.**

Our models, teachers, and partners in this historic undertaking are America's best-run companies — companies that led the quality revolution of the past two decades — companies like GE, Harley Davidson, and Motorola, which have kept America competitive in the world market. They have already been through the transformation from industrial-age to information-age management. They have been through the learning curve, they have made the mistakes and fixed them, all while dealing with the risks of a free market.

Their time is valuable, and we value it. Their advice is not just theory; it is tried and true. We gratefully acknowledge their many contributions in the following pages. And we are also acknowledging their contributions the best way I know how — by taking their advice and examples to heart, and putting them into practice.

Most of what successful businesses, and now government, have learned can be summed up in two principles: focus on customers, and listen to workers. Old-fashioned bureaucracies focus on hierarchy and listen for instructions from the top. Doing otherwise is a big change.

We are making the big change. Here are some examples:

- The smallest federal civilian workforce in over 30 years, down by 309,000 (as of January 1997) from the 2,200,000 on the payroll when we took office.

- A big reduction in red tape and government bureaucracy — leading to savings of $132 billion for the taxpayer.

- Easier access to government agencies using information technology.

- A marked change in the philosophy of regulatory agencies from an adversarial approach to a more cooperative — and effective — method.

- A new spirit in government, in which creativity and innovation are rewarded, not frowned upon.

It is my pleasure in this book to play straight man (a role for which I have special qualifications) to Dilbert — and to his creator, Scott Adams. I want Americans to know that government reinvention is happening. My thanks to Dilbert and Scott for making the story of government reinvention more fun.

> **The federal civilian workforce is the smallest it's been in over 30 years.**

In the following pages, you'll see what else is happening. I hope you enjoy reading about what government is learning from the best in business. President Clinton has set as our performance goal to be every bit as good as the best in business. We've made real progress, but we still have a ways to go. When all of government reaches the goal, all of America will be proud.

Al Gore

BUSINESSLIKE GOVERNMENT

CHAPTER 2
Taxpayers Are Customers Too
Business teaches government about customer service

Customer? What's a Customer?

People used to say that if government were a diner, it would be closed for lunch.

There are reasons for that.

Over the past 60 years, government got bigger and bigger. Laws and regulations multiplied. Small departments became complex bureaucracies.

It wasn't easy to focus on the customer. Most federal workers were trapped in an industrial-age assembly line where they passed paper from one office to the next. "Customers" were rarely seen or thought about. Even the word was rarely used.

So it's not surprising that many federal workers lost sight of the fact that their services were ultimately meant to benefit the American public.

BUSINESSLIKE GOVERNMENT

Too many people began to feel the whole government was like one big "no help whatsoever" desk.

DILBERT reprinted by permission of United Feature Syndicate, Inc.

Used to Abuse

For a long time, Americans have been unhappy with many government services. Of course, not everyone in the private sector was doing things right, either. Waiting in a long line at the bank or not being able to get a straight answer over the phone was just as frustrating as having to take a day off to visit a government office.

Customers were starved for attention and used to abuse.

Then something happened.

In the face of the information explosion and global competition, American business underwent its own revolution.

Customers Rule

Corporations spent 10 painful years reengineering to put the customer at the center of their activities. To succeed, companies now must offer their customers variety, quality, convenience, and excellent service. They do this by listening to customers, empowering employees, controlling costs, and using information technology.

Now banks have 24-hour phone service and ATMs. Visa sends replacement cards with just a phone call. Nordstrom fixes complaints on the spot. New cars seldom break down. Service shops give you a ride to the bus stop.

In short, America's leading companies stopped taking customers for granted.

Listening to Business

Government, too, needed to learn how to become customer friendly. But first it had to get over a myth: that government and business were so different that they had nothing to learn from each other. The truth is, nearly all the tools and techniques that helped American companies get back on their feet could be adapted to make government work better.

In June 1993, Vice President Gore invited top executives from Cadillac, Ritz-Carlton, The Limited, and other companies to join him at Congress Hall in Philadelphia for the Summit Conference on Reinventing Government. He listened as these managers emphasized a common

Standards Equal to the Best in Business

theme: Put the customer first. This message came up again and again, in dozens of other meetings with executives from such companies as Motorola, Southwest Airlines, and Saturn, as well as a Who's Who of management experts.

Lessons from that conference led to President Clinton's 1993 order [see below] for "a revolution within the federal government" to change the way it does business. The order requires agencies to identify their customers, ask them what they want, and then set standards equal to the best in business.

President Clinton's Executive Order 12862
"Setting Customer Service Standards"

Embark on a revolution within the Federal Government.

- Identify customers who are, or should be, served by the agency.
- Survey customers to determine the kind and quality of services they want and their level of satisfaction with existing services.
- Post service standards and measure results against them.
- Benchmark customer service standards against the best in business.
- Provide customers with choices in both the sources of service and means of delivery.
- Make information, services, and complaint systems easily accessible.
- Provide means to address customer complaints.

The standard of quality shall be equal to the best in business.

Evangelists of Customer Service

In response to the President's order, 400 government workers met at Hunt Valley, Maryland, with 40 executives from Disney, Federal Express, Xerox, and other companies known for their customer focus.

They learned how Disney executives, including Judson Green, President of Walt Disney Attractions, spend time in their theme parks dressed up as Mickey, Donald, or Goofy — so they can learn first-hand about their customers.

They heard how Ralph Stayer, CEO of Johnsonville Foods, let production workers decide whether sausage tasted good enough to ship — so each employee would take responsibility for customers.

Finally, they accepted a challenge thrown down by Tom Peters, management expert, to become "raging inexorable thunderlizard evangelists of customer service."

In search of excellence.

DILBERT reprinted by permission of United Feature Syndicate, Inc.

Changing Everything

The Hunt Valley Conference was the first of hundreds of joint activities with business that are moving the federal government steadily away from its "no help whatsoever" image.

Large customer-focused companies are:

- running workshops for government employees;

- working with government agencies to transfer know-how in areas as diverse as inventory management and video training; and

- participating in benchmarking studies across a range of topics such as handling complaints and running a 1-800 telephone service.

The best companies know it's no simple matter to become a first-class, customer-driven organization. Doing that means holding a big mirror up to the organization, acknowledging what's there, and then changing what needs fixing. Sometimes, that means changing everything.

Uncle Sam Delivers

Agencies are changing. They are asking their customers what they want, listening to the answers, and promising to deliver. Instead of blindly following procedural rules, employees are getting flexibility to use their heads to meet customer needs. However, everyone isn't born knowing how to serve customers. So, most agencies are offering customer service training. One of the stars is FEMA, where all full time and disaster relief employees have taken customer service behavioral skills training.

Across government, agencies that focus on customer service are showing improvement. For example:

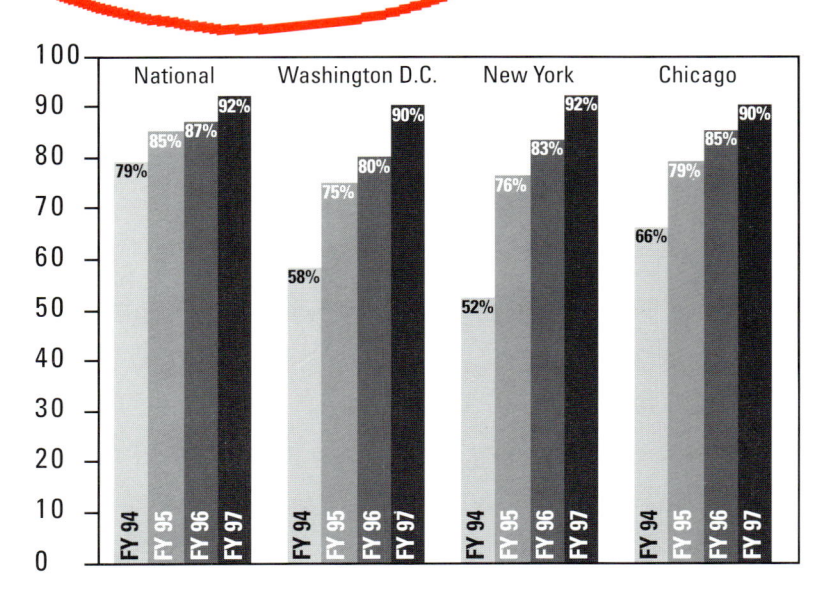

- 91 percent of visitors to the National Parks in 1996 rated their overall satisfaction as "very good" or "good" on services including lodging, food, facilities, exhibits, ranger programs, campgrounds, and picnic areas.

- Social Security now fills 97 percent of social security card requests within five days.

- The Postal Service is delivering 92 percent of First-Class Mail on time — up from 79 percent in fiscal year 1994.

The Postal Service is delivering 92 percent of First-Class Mail on time — up from 79 percent in FY 1994.

	FY 94	FY 95	FY 96	FY 97
National	79%	85%	87%	92%
Washington D.C.	58%	75%	80%	90%
New York	52%	76%	83%	92%
Chicago	66%	79%	85%	90%

BUSINESSLIKE GOVERNMENT

REINVENTION ZONE INTERVIEW

This year, 570 government organizations are publishing customer service standards and working like crazy to deliver.

To Beat Wal-Mart

Consider the case of Brigadier General Kenneth Privratsky, Commander of Defense Distribution Region East (DDRE), who entered The Reinvention Zone to discover the secrets of Delta Air Lines, Caterpillar, IBM, and Wal-Mart.

Q: DDRE does what?

A: DDRE distributes everything from battle tanks to toothpaste for our customers — most of the U.S. military forces.

Q: How big is your operation?

A: I have 8,000 employees in 13 depots who fulfill 15 million orders per year.

Q: Why did you go to the private sector for help?

A: I knew our customer service was much slower than the private sector's. So I sent teams to visit our civilian counterparts — aviation depots went to Delta Air Lines, the heavy equipment depot went to Caterpillar, et cetera. My staff went to IBM, Wal-Mart, Eddie Bauer, and Spiegel.

I sent teams to visit Delta Air Lines, Caterpillar, Eddie Bauer, and Spiegel.

Q: How did the companies react?
A: Everybody was eager to share their ideas.

Q: What did you learn?
A: We learned four things. First, ask your customers what they want, and give it to them. Second, raise standards — our orders took four days; the private sector took one. Third, cut management — our supervisor-employee ratio was 1:10; theirs was 1:20. Finally, cross-train staff to meet changing demands.

Q: What surprised you most?
A: Companies' performance standards for the individual worker were simply much higher. Now we aim higher.

Q: How much has DDRE changed since you saw Wal-Mart?
A: Pretty much everything changed. Routine orders now take us a day instead of four. We've reached a 1:15 supervisor-employee ratio. We review our workload daily and adjust for the next day. Before, incredibly, we did it only once a month.

Q: What's the bottom line?
A: Our performance is better in every category — we saved more than $28 million. That money goes directly to improving military readiness.

Q: What's your next goal?
A: To beat Wal-Mart.

Zoning in on the needs of the small business customer.

DILBERT reprinted by permission of United Feature Syndicate, Inc.

TALES FROM THE REINVENTION ZONE

The Loan Arranger
Ex-Im is getting loans to small businesses through partnerships with private banks.

A helping hand for small business

One of the toughest tasks for small business exporters is to find "working capital" — money to buy inventory and raw materials. Reinvention at the Export-Import Bank has provided easier access to funds.

Ex-Im, as it's called, is a government agency set up to promote U.S. exports. Until recently, its services have benefited mostly large exporters.

> **Small business exporters can borrow money for working capital.**

Now, Ex-Im has found a way to better serve a key group of its potential customers — America's 128,000 small and medium-sized exporters. The Delegated Authority Program allows it to leverage working capital loans to small businesses through partnerships with private banks.

Through delegated authority, Ex-Im Bank can guarantee 90 percent of the loans that local lenders extend to exporters, without case-by-case approval from Washington. Certain qualified lenders can extend up to $5 million in loans per exporter. Lenders like the program because it reduces their risk — yet provides them with a new product to offer customers. Small business is happy to have this new — and more accessible — source of funds.

One CEO who has benefited from the new program is Warren Fuller, head of Paul O. Abbe, Inc., a family-owned business in New Jersey with over $7 million in sales in 1996. The company manufactures processing equipment for chemicals and pharmaceuticals. It employs over 40 skilled workers, such as chemical and mechanical engineers.

Fuller learned about the program through his local bank, the First National Bank of New England. First National has used delegated authority to finance $22 million of

> *"Delegated authority has created over $1 billion in export — and many U.S. jobs."*
>
> **Michael Selfridge**
> VP for International Banking
> Silicon Valley Bank

working capital loans to small businesses. It extended a $200,000 line of credit for export-related working capital to Fuller's company. This money enabled him to finance six projects — which led to more than $1.5 million in new sales.

"Ex-Im is leveraging its resources by bringing in commercial banks who know the customer," says Fuller. "Without this program, it would have been almost impossible to pay for the steel and other working capital we needed for exports. Work-in-process is very difficult to collateralize, and banks consider foreign accounts receivables as taboo. Also, my bank gives me 24-hour service. Ex-Im itself just isn't set up to handle a small customer like me."

The program benefits the banks too. "We view exports as the main driver of growth for small and medium-sized business," says Michael Selfridge, Vice President for International Banking of Silicon Valley Bank in California, which serves fast-growing, high-tech businesses around the United States.

"The advantage of this program is that we can approve loans directly, without prior authorization from Washington. That means we can serve our customers promptly and take a limited risk where we feel it will pay off. We've used delegated authority to finance some $135 million in working capital loans, which has created over $1 billion in exports — and many U.S. jobs," says Selfridge. "It's a phenomenal success story."

By partnering with 80 local banks in 42 states, Ex-Im has been able to double its lending to small business — from 155 loans totaling $180.6 million in 1994 to 286 loans totaling $377.8 million in 1996 — without adding staff in Washington.

"The old Ex-Im Bank was not relevant to me," says Warren Fuller. "But this is an example of how reinvented government can help small business."

> *"...this is an example of how reinvented government can help small business."*
>
> **Warren Fuller**
> CEO and President, Paul O. Abbe, Inc.

Social Security Answers the Call

Private-sector techniques have helped the Social Security Administration speed information to customers.

Toll-free, hassle-free Social Security

Social Security provides almost 50 million individuals with retirement, survivors, disability, or welfare income. That kind of customer base generates a lot of questions. In 1995, 121 million calls were placed to Social Security's toll-free number, but only 44 million callers got through and were served. Even with about 4,500 people answering the phone, phone access was so poor that many people just couldn't get the help they needed. Today if you dial 1-800-772-1213, it's a different story.

"We wanted to improve, but we didn't know which efforts would give us the biggest bang for the buck," says Toni Lenane, Senior Advisor to the SSA Commissioner.

The breakthrough came when Social Security reevaluated its strategy for service delivery and decided to talk to customers directly about their expectations. In 1995 the agency joined a telephone benchmarking study sponsored by the National Performance Review. This study compared toll-free number services in the public sector (including the IRS, Bureau of the Census, and Immigration and Naturalization Service) to leading private-sector companies, including:

> "I was very impressed by Social Security's strong commitment to making great customer service fundamental to how government does business."
>
> **Judson Green**
> President, Walt Disney Attractions

- American Express Travel Related Services
- AT&T Universal Card Services
- Bell Canada
- Citibank
- Duke Power Company
- GE Answer Center
- Saturn Corporation
- USAA Insurance

The benchmarking study demonstrated how successful companies manage large phone banks — and helped Social Security fix its problem.

"It was important to learn from the benchmarking. We were trying to reinvent the wheel until we looked at industry, which had already spent years refining the process," says Lenane. "We learned that in the private sector, training is followed by a student-mentor environment so there is always someone more experienced to ask. Also, training continues on an as-needed basis so the operators' skills and information are always up-to-date."

"Private companies train the person answering the phone to offer the customer a full range of assistance," Lenane adds. "We were doing just the opposite. For instance, before this exercise, the person who answered the 800 number at Social Security couldn't take a claim. That meant callers would have to wait about three weeks for their local office to call them back and take their claim."

In just 18 months, Social Security almost doubled its telephone answering capacity without adding new hires. The agency did this, first, by working with AT&T to design a new network that provided the capacity and automated features found in the best toll-free business services. Second, it reinvented the way it records employers' reports of wages through extra reliance on information technology; the people who had been operating the old system then went to work answering the phones on the toll-free service. Third, it trained other people in the organization to help out at peak times.

Now that people could get to Social Security when they called the toll-free number, the agency took the next step customers wanted: It started to train telephone operators to take claims immediately — over the toll-free number.

According to Lenane, "We have made great gains in delivering toll-free telephone service, but we know that to be truly world-class, we need to continuously improve to meet changing customer needs and expectations. Our operational people continue to learn, test, and implement new approaches that bode well for future success."

> "We were trying to reinvent the wheel until we looked at industry — which had already spent years refining the process."
>
> **Toni Lenane**
> Social Security Administration

From Trails to Sales

The National Park Service and Forest Service serve their customers right in the REI store.

Cooperating with REI

Few retailers could imagine showcasing federal employees in their stores. But that's what's happening in Seattle, where a major sporting goods retailer has teamed up with the National Park Service and the Forest Service to offer customers a direct link to government information — while they shop.

REI is the nation's leading retail cooperative, with more than 1.4 million active members and $484 million in annual sales of outdoor gear. REI's innovative flagship store in Seattle encompasses 80,000 square feet (not including a small forest with hiking and biking trails) and draws 2.5 million visitors a year.

One of the store's greatest innovations was created when the Park Service and Forest Service moved their offices from a downtown federal building to a booth right in the REI store. From this spot — called the Outdoor Recreation Information Center, or ORIC — rangers provide information on park openings and closings, trail and river conditions, campsites, and more.

Before the move, the office was only open on weekdays and served about 62,000 customers each year. At the new location, with extended hours on weekends and evenings, the volume of business has at least doubled. On peak days, employees serve 600 customers.

The shift not only puts the rangers where the customers are, but it also saves the government a significant sum in office costs. REI charges the Forest and Park services only minimal rent, about enough to cover incidental expenses. "I consider this a blended operation. We share phone lines, storage space, even customer service training," says John Sheppard, the store's operations manager.

The advantages for both sides are clear, Sheppard adds. "We have learned a lot. The Park Service and Forest Service have access to information that REI staff could not get easily. The rangers, in turn, have learned from us about dealing with high volumes of customers. I can't put it in exact dollars, but I know that ORIC has been a financial benefit to our store. We get tremendous, positive feedback. The thing is, their customers are our customers."

What's Next?

Thousands of companies are helping agencies get to know and serve their customers. The challenge ahead is to carry the customer service message throughout the federal government.

CHAPTER 3
Creative License
Unleashing the creative power of government employees

The Earthquake

A new idea is shaking up government.

Business calls it "empowerment," "leveraging employees," or "investing in human resources." It's the terribly simple idea that people can think.

"People are smart, people have tremendous capacity, and it is our job not to give them power but to let them use the power they already have," Suzanne Allford, then-Vice President of Wal-Mart, told Vice President Gore at the Reinvention Summit. "Employee involvement is the secret of our success."

Many of America's top companies have been rocked by this new idea. For most of this century, business focused on structural position — market share, brand franchise, cost structure, and so forth. But in the past 10 years, companies with the "people can think" idea — like Southwest Airlines, Thermo Electron, and Banc One — have come out of nowhere to shake up stodgy industries and challenge established leaders.

DILBERT reprinted by permission of United Feature Syndicate, Inc.

The source of their competitive advantage? When companies push responsibility down toward front-line employees, decisions can be made faster and better because those employees are closer to the market.

And new ideas percolate in such environments. Companies that have empowered employees — including Hewlett-Packard, GE, IBM, and Merck — have been strong enough to weather storms that sank many of their competitors.

Industry has taken this lesson to heart. But for government? It's like an earthquake. In fact, in this chapter, you will read about an actual earthquake that isolated some federal employees from their bosses — and they responded by becoming more productive. A kind of virtual

CREATIVE LICENSE

> **Panel 1:** "I've been saying for years that 'employees are our most valuable asset.'"
>
> **Panel 2:** "It turns out that I was wrong. Money is our most valuable asset. Employees are ninth."
>
> **Panel 3:** "I'm afraid to ask what came in eighth." "Carbon paper."

DILBERT reprinted by permission of United Feature Syndicate, Inc.

earthquake is shaking up the comfortable status quo of government hierarchy. It is changing management's perspective on the value and virtue of their employees.

Employees are the Government's Most Valuable Asset

For a long time, many government workers felt as though they were in a Dilbert cartoon. They were imprisoned in a system where they had little power and no one listened to their ideas. Decisions were made so many levels above them that it seemed futile trying to change things.

So it comes as no surprise that the CEOs zeroed in on this problem. They told Vice President Gore: Your employees are your best asset. Start using them.

Involve the Workers

No organization — public or private — can change unless the people doing the jobs are involved. Without this, directives from above just fill up the office wastebaskets.

> "The essence of employee involvement is employee trust."
>
> **Vaughn Beals**
> Former CEO, Harley Davidson

Vaughn Beals proved this point. He took over Harley Davidson when the company was only a few months away from financial collapse. The reason for these dire straits was best captured in a widely distributed photo of new Harleys in a showroom, cardboard under each to catch leaking oil.

"We removed multiple layers of management. We cut [headquarters] staff," said Beals. "We moved to employee involvement. The essence of employee involvement is employee trust. We told each employee, you make it, you inspect it, you analyze the inspection data statistically, you decide if it's good, you adjust your machine. We trust you."

Every corporate executive at the Reinvention Summit told the Vice President that the energy, creativity, and innovative ideas that turned their companies into world-class competitors came directly from their own employees. Union representatives, too, played a crucial role in the transformations. From the perspective of business, the most obvious way to improve government was to invest in its prime asset: its employees.

Listen and Learn

It's easy to espouse such principles as "listen to workers" and "let workers work." It's harder to put them into practice. These goals need to be backed up by a system that encourages workers to speak up and come forward with their suggestions.

Too often, large organizations are set up to get existing tasks done in a certain way, and people with vested interests may oppose any break in the normal pattern. Employees learn to do as they are told, even if they have better ideas.

Some employee ideas are discouraged quickly by managers who believe they already know the best methods. After all, managers are traditionally selected for being smart and aggressive. The natural inclination of such people is to want things done their way. For many of them, it isn't easy to say, "Let's try it your way."

Other employee ideas simply disappear into "suggestion programs" and are never heard of again. Processing times for employee suggestions sometimes last longer than the employees themselves.

Reengineering to Empower

Companies have spent years reengineering their entire work flows to make room for innovation and improvement. Now, government is playing catch-up — but that means it can benefit from the advice of those who learned through trial and error.

Businesses that were able to make a "culture change" typically worked on several areas at the same time: rewarding performance, reducing overhead, scrapping unnecessary rules and regulations, intrapreneurship, and training. By applying these principles, government is finding that it too can unlock the potential of its employees.

Government has made progress in all these areas. For example:

- *Rewarding performance.* The Vice President uses the Hammer Award — a $6 hammer wrapped in ribbons and mounted on a plaque — to support and reward innovative approaches to government. Just as top-level recognition has been an essential tool in creating the best private companies, the Hammer Award program has encouraged federal workers to come forward with innovations to improve efficiency. To date, NPR has given Hammer Awards to more than 900 teams comprising more than 10,000 workers.

> **Some agencies have followed the example of GE and Harley Davidson and reduced their headquarters by one-third or more.**

- *Reducing overhead.* Agencies have restructured, cutting out layers of excess supervisory and administrative personnel. Between January 1993 and 1997, the federal civilian workforce was trimmed by 309,000. Some agencies — notably the General Services Administration, the Office of Personnel Management, the Department of Interior, and U.S. Customs — have followed the example of GE and Harley Davidson and reduced their headquarters by one-third or more.

- *Scrapping unnecessary rules and regulations.* A top priority has been to free government workers from over-regulation. Agencies have scrapped more than 640,000 pages of internal rules and regulations that advertised distrust of workers and sapped their enthusiasm and initiative.

- *Intrapreneurship.* Pockets of reformers who are experimenting with innovative approaches to government have been designated "reinvention laboratories." This entitles them to special help from the Vice President's office in cutting through red tape and testing out new ideas. Many of the experiments are spreading far beyond the organizations that developed them.

- *Training.* Frank Doyle of General Electric told the government, "Empowerment is a disorderly gesture unless people are given the tools and knowledge that self-direction demands." Government is just beginning to get the message that it needs to invest in its employees and train them well — as the private sector does. Some agencies, such as Social Security, have teamed up with leading corporations to learn how to use training better.

> "Empowerment is a disorderly gesture unless people are given the tools and knowledge that self-direction demands."
>
> **Frank Doyle**
> Executive VP, General Electric
> 1993

CREATIVE LICENSE

REINVENTION ZONE INTERVIEW

The Right Stuff

Consider the case of Anne Williams, Mission Director for the U.S. Agency for International Development (USAID)/Senegal. Williams trusted her employees to make the right decisions — and wonderful things are happening.

Q. What does USAID do in Senegal?

A. USAID is supporting efforts to improve natural resource management, health care, and market liberalization with an emphasis on empowering women and working at the local level.

Q. How did you change things?

A. When I arrived in 1994, USAID/Senegal was a very traditional, hierarchical — and frustrating — organization. Based on what I had seen work in my 13 years as a corporate and government lawyer, I did two things. First, I encouraged the mission to reorganize into multifunctional teams and then delegated responsibility to those teams. Second, I introduced the idea of customer focus.

Q. What happened?

A. First, I had to gain peoples' confidence and trust. My management style is very hands-off. I like to set guidelines and leave the details to the people who are closest to the work. But I came into a organization that was extremely centralized. For example, every international phone call had to have the director's permission. Now I give each team a budget, and they decide for themselves how to allocate the money — for travel, office administration, training, et cetera. Even more important, each team has the responsibility to make the program decisions to obtain the agreed-upon result.

Q. What has been the most difficult challenge?

A. The most difficult aspect of this philosophy has been to fully empower the local Senegalese employees of USAID. These people are absolutely crucial because they are the continuity. They stay, whereas the Americans leave after a few years. So now, for the first time, a Senegalese woman is managing our entire health care program.

> **I give each team a budget, and they decide for themselves how to allocate the money.**

> *If you give someone the responsibility, they will rise to it, and often exceed your expectations.*

Q. You mentioned empowerment. Can you explain why it works?

A. Empowerment works on two levels: the organizational and the individual. When I first arrived here, I could have imposed my own framework for reorganizing the mission. But instead, we got the whole mission together and they designed the reorganization themselves. They were freed to use their imaginations and to completely lead the process. The result is far better than anything I could have done on my own.

Second, empowerment succeeds at the individual level. Here's an example: We are currently developing a new strategy. The strategy team decided to put two local employees in charge of conducting focus groups with the customers and partners — a brand-new initiative. I myself would not necessarily have chosen these two individuals for the task, but I was wrong. They have done a wonderful job on this project and have improved as well in their regular job performance. These two people are up for awards.

It shows that if you give someone the responsibility, they will rise to it, and often exceed your expectations.

Tales from the Reinvention Zone

Employee Powered

When one government worker set out to improve customer service for a veterans office, he turned to IBM and AT&T — not for equipment, but for ideas.

"Before we started, if you looked at our internal statistics on performance, we were doing a great job," says Joe Thompson, a Vietnam veteran who runs the Department of Veterans Affairs benefits office in New York. But when he asked the customers — veterans — he heard a different story.

"Veterans were unhappy with the whole way we were structured," he says. "We were set up like an assembly line, with 25 steps to process a disability claim. When a veteran phoned in for information, he would speak to someone outside this process — who could never answer the question. It was enormously frustrating. Our staff — many of whom are veterans themselves — really wanted to help people. But the system was set up in a way that didn't give them the chance."

Thompson knew the VA office had to change to serve its customers. So he used successful businesses as a model.

"In April 1993, VA designated us as a reinvention lab," he said. "That gave us the freedom to be experimental. We went to IBM and AT&T and saw that we needed to change everything — our organizational structure, work flow, job descriptions, performance measurement, and compensation systems. It was a big job. But in four years, we've done all that. In business terminology we actually 'reengineered' our operation — though frankly none of us had ever heard the word before."

The biggest change? Employees took charge.

"We used IBM's Organizational Systems Design Model," Thompson explains. "We created self-managing teams, eliminated half the supervisory positions, and shortened the claim process from 25 to 8 steps. We adopted the 'balanced scorecard' approach to measure performance, and we added in measures of customer satisfaction and employee development. Now we're trying to replace civil service pay scales with skill-based pay, so our employees can be rewarded for what they contribute."

"The process was hardly smooth," he adds. "Along the way, all scenarios that could go wrong did. We had to learn from our mistakes. But the result is worth it:

> "In business terminology, we actually 'reengineered' our operation."
>
> **Joe Thompson**
> VA, New York

Personnel costs are down 25 percent, and call-back volume has been reduced through better service. Customer surveys show that veterans think we are faster and more responsive. What I'm most proud of is that we all did it together, and every single employee played a significant role."

A Uniformly Good Idea

A common-sense suggestion from a front-line employee is saving $220,000 annually for a Marine Corps supply operation.

Phil Archuleta, an employee at the Marine Corps Recruit Depot in San Diego, noticed that the Depot was issuing a lot of extra-large size uniforms to new, overweight recruits. But Marine Corps boot camp has a way of making people lose weight. Within a few weeks, practically all the recruits dropped down enough to exchange the XL's for a smaller size. Regulations prohibited the Marines from reissuing the barely used XL uniforms — because, of course, they had already been issued once. The Marines had to give away perfectly good uniforms — some never worn at all — to government surplus stores.

Archuleta suggested that the Marines could *wash* the uniforms and then reissue them to incoming overweight recruits. His common-sense idea saved the depot $89,000 in the first five months and $220,000 over a year.

Empowerment By The Gallon

Employees in a government paint supply office are using private-sector forecasting software to reduce on-shelf inventory and cut costs dramatically.

The General Services Administration's Auburn paints and chemicals center has reorganized to empower its workforce. "We used to be the typical government office," says Jim Hamilton, the manager who led the reorganization. "Before, nobody could make a decision on their own. Everything was controlled by centralized rules and constraints."

"So we took a different approach. First, we gave our people the right tools. We trained all our desk managers to use a vendor-managed inventory system just like GE's. Then we gave them each a set of targets, with total freedom to decide how to achieve these targets. All kinds of inventory control decisions like ordering and markups that used to be dictated from my office are now at the disposal of local desk managers."

> "We trained all our desk managers to use a vendor-managed inventory system just like GE's."
>
> **Jim Hamilton**
> GSA, Auburn Center

The results are great, he says. "Our employees are much more motivated, and we're saving on inventory costs. Instead of keeping $40 million worth of inventory on the shelves, we keep $8 million. Think of all that inventory like milk in your refrigerator — it's got a shelf life, and after a certain point you have to recycle."

Shaking Up Government

An earthquake literally left bosses and workers on opposite sides of a divide — and productivity soared.

"It was pitch black and the noise was incredible. It just roared through," recalls Janice Peck about that early morning in January 1994, when the Northridge Earthquake struck Los Angeles. "The freeway bridge over the I-5, just south of Valencia where I live, collapsed and cut us off 30 miles from the main VA benefits office in West L.A."

But Peck and her coworkers, some of whom lived another 45 miles to the north, were determined to stay on the job. "We started using the Angeles Crest Highway, the mountain road," says Monique Koslow. "It was taking three hours — and then the snow came and cut off that option. The first night, it took four and a half hours to get home." She wondered how long she could keep up the exhausting commute.

She needn't have worried, according to her coworker and carpooler, Bill Parker: "Our director moved very quickly." Within 10 days, all three were settled in a telecommuting center that the General Services Administration created from scratch after the quake. "I give a lot of credit to FEMA, too," Parker continues. The Federal Emergency Management Agency "got us some computers so we could get up and running, and they paid for our whole first year of operation — rent, supplies, clerical support, everything."

The three are disability rating specialists; they review veterans' claims and medical records and decide eligibility for benefits — a job that can be done in nearly any quiet place. It is perfect work for a telecommuter.

The Valencia telecommuting center was supposed to be a temporary solution, just until the freeways were repaired. "But we started plotting right away about how to stay here," says Peck. "Actually, years ago, when I started as a rating specialist with VA in West L.A., a couple of us realized we could do the work better outside of the office. We proposed it to the management, and they said 'No, we won't be able to watch you.'" Traditional managers can't help imagining the worst.

"So we offered them a bribe," she says. "We said we'd do 10 percent more work if we could work at home. They

> **"We are 12 percent of the regional office disability rating specialists, and we produce 17 percent of all the ratings."**
>
> Bill Parker
> VA, Los Angeles

bought that and then asked headquarters in Washington, who said 'No, you can't let them work independently.' Our promise of extra work didn't interest Washington."

But the earthquake let them make good on their offer. Parker has the statistics to prove it. "We are 12 percent of the regional office disability rating specialists, and we produce 17 percent of all the ratings. But that's not the whole story. Some veteran claims take longer than others. A veteran's first claim takes longer to review because we have to evaluate service medical records as well as any current medical problems. We do 19 percent of all first claims. And the most time-consuming category of first-time claims are those with eight or more medical or emotional issues. We do 47 percent of those."

How does the team explain its superior productivity? "Not so many interruptions," says Peck. "Downtown, the phones are ringing and people are talking, asking you questions, and the supervisors are always changing your priorities — telling you to drop whatever you're working on and work on something else. Here, we get a box of cases and we just do them. The sooner we get done, the sooner the veterans get their money."

CREATIVE LICENSE

Stew Liff, the regional director, has taken the Valencia success seriously. By next year, he plans to begin relocating many workers who serve veterans from the regional office to four area VA medical centers.

The Valencia telecommuting team is leading the way. Peck says, "Our team is producing the work. Our quality is good. We plan our own vacation times, report our leave, and cover for each other when someone's sick. We're responsible adults and we're capable of doing all that without management."

All it took was an earthquake.

DILBERT reprinted by permission of United Feature Syndicate, Inc.

CHAPTER 4

Cutting Waste and Red Tape
Making taxpayers' money go further

Government doesn't actually have a form for requesting a drink of water. Never did. But there were forms and rules and procedures for everything else, or so it seemed to most everyone — inside or outside the federal government. Government has most of the same management problems as the rest of society, but it downright invented red tape:

> **red tape** *n.* Official forms and procedures, especially when oppressively complex and time consuming. [From its former use in tying British official documents]
>
> — American Heritage Dictionary, Third Edition, Houghton Mifflin, 1992

Government employees filled out forms constantly. There were forms for getting permission to use a can of spray paint that had passed its shelf-life expiration date. Forms for reporting what subway stop you got off at. And forms for getting a day of vacation.

The same was true for people who had to deal with the government. The Internal Revenue Service alone had more than 600 forms and sets of instructions for its customers. Before the Small Business Administration reinvented its processes, it used to take 100 pages of paperwork to apply for a loan that now requires a single piece of paper.

Every Problem Started as a Solution

The red tape had a certain logic. Government bought a lot, and it was difficult to make sure every business had a fair chance to bid for contracts. And government spent tax dollars. It had to be sure that incompetent workers didn't waste them or dishonest workers didn't steal them.

But the red tape hasn't worked out quite the way it was meant to.

Efforts to protect the taxpayers against incompetents or crooks wound up wasting money, not saving it.

DILBERT reprinted by permission of United Feature Syndicate, Inc.

Red Tape Was Everywhere

Government may have invented red tape, but its exclusive patent ran out long ago. Corporations added rules, procedures, and checkers as they grew. Private-sector workers have felt the same kinds of distrust and bureaucracy as government workers. Dilbert could have worked for the government, but he doesn't. He works for corporate America.

But corporate America started to change. The shock of losing great chunks of market share in autos — the symbol of American industrial supremacy — to the Japanese woke the private sector up.

Giant corporations saw they were wasting a large part of their human potential and their cash through red tape and distrust. By the mid-1980s, many Fortune 500 companies had started trusting workers and cutting the red tape that bound them.

Listening to Business

Many companies were very generous in explaining to government how they had cut waste and red tape. They helped to devise a three-point strategy to fight waste and red tape in government:

- Change from headquarters: cutting and simplifying rules that require extra steps or that force delays.

> **The Army now buys duffel bags for $2.29 each instead of $6.75. It all adds up.**

- Change from the front line: giving people the freedom to come forward with new ideas — and to try them — while rewarding workers for successful innovation instead of penalizing them for making mistakes.

- Change from the outside: bringing in outside expertise in streamlining, reengineering, and changing workplace culture.

There have been some major successes. Besides reducing the workforce by 309,000 as of January 1997 and scrapping more than 640,000 pages of internal rules and regulations, the most notable success has been reform of the greatest red tape factory of them all: government procurement.

The entire system is being overhauled, with huge help from Congress in the form of the Federal Acquisition Streamlining Act of 1994 and the Clinger-Cohen Act of 1996. The Pentagon has gone to multi-year contracts and is using more commercial parts. That is saving $2.7 billion on the new C-17 cargo plane and $2.9 billion on new smart munitions. Smaller purchases count, too. For example, the Army now buys duffel bags for $2.29 each instead of $6.75. It all adds up.

The government used to make small purchases — a stapler, a book, a piece of software — just like it made big ones: with paperwork costing $50 or more. The cost to the government was ridiculous — a $4 stapler wound up costing $54, and it could take months for the forms to be filled out before the stapler got to the person who needed it. The vendors weren't very happy either, waiting two to three months to get their Treasury check for four dollars.

Way back in 1985, five Department of Commerce employees were working on how to streamline small purchases. They came up with an overpoweringly common-sensical idea from the private sector: a credit card. In a pilot program with Rocky Mountain BankCard System, Visa cards were issued to 500 employees. It was, not surprisingly, a success, and in 1993 the National Performance Review recommended that the program be greatly expanded. To date the government has used the cards over 10 million times to buy goods and services worth $20 billion — saving over $700 million so far and speeding delivery of needed tools to workers.

All told, procurement reform has saved the taxpayers over $12 billion to date.

Procurement reform has saved the taxpayers over $12 billion to date.

REINVENTION ZONE INTERVIEW

Commercial Space

Consider the case of Donna Shirley, the Earthling in charge of exploring Mars. She manages the Mars exploration program at the Jet Propulsion Laboratory (JPL).

Q. These must be exciting times for NASA and JPL, just like the old days.

A. Right. Things are exciting the way they used to be. But science is no longer king. It's money — period.

Q. Is that a complaint about budget cuts?

A. No, no, I'm not complaining. The budgets per mission are small, but we have an ongoing program of missions every 26 months. It's great — just like 1970, when I worked on Mariner 10. Back then, we had an immovable spending cap, and our contractor, Boeing, knew there wasn't any more money — no matter what. We had a small, young, tight-knit team; you couldn't tell who worked for Boeing or who worked for JPL. And we had a tight schedule, too: three years to build and launch. That all makes for creativity. That's the way things are again with Lockheed Martin and our mission to Mars.

Q. But don't tight budgets compromise the mission?

A. No. Because we don't have to do everything with a single mission, every mission can be cheaper. We put Sojourner up there and drove her around gathering data for the same money Hollywood spent making *Waterworld*. And we got better reviews. Next year, we're having a 2-for-1 sale. Two Martian missions for the price of one Pathfinder. Engineers are smart people, and they thrive on challenge. Just tell them what the parameters are, including the budget, and they'll do it for you.

Q. So balancing the federal budget should spark creativity all over the government?

A. There's more to it than that. To get that kind of creativity from a team, you can't have hierarchy; you have to have a kind of intimacy — a partnership — or the team just won't spark. And that means the whole team, private contractors included. I've written a book about it; you can find it on the World Wide Web at *managingcreativity.com.*

Q. Nice plug. What private contractors are on your team?

A. IBM, for example, came to us with a very fast, low-cost, commercial computer that uses regular software. Its speed let us do a lot of stuff in space without fancy programming. And then we could design the ground station around commercial-type software and hardware, too. That alone saved us about $25 million.

> **Two Martian missions for the price of one Pathfinder.**

And now IBM has a space-certified computer that it can sell to future space missions.

Motorola's a partner too, although it was leery at first. We needed a modem for Sojourner to talk to the lander. To design and build one would have cost millions that we didn't have. We thought Motorola's $300 commercial modem might work if we spent a few hundred thousand dollars adapting it for space. Motorola wasn't so sure it wanted to risk its good name like that. Essentially, it said that if we took the modem to Mars, it was out of warranty.

Q. Any other companies help you get to Mars?
A. Our main partner is Lockheed Martin. Our partnership's most recent success is the spacecraft that just entered Mars orbit. It will circle Mars for two years, making a detailed map of the surface, tracking Martian weather, and gathering other information that we need. And then comes Stardust, a probe to gather particles from a comet and bring them back to Earth. You see, we plan on having a long-term partnership with Lockheed Martin. That way, it can set up a production line and invest in research. And there's no game playing, no overruns and bailouts, like there used to be. The company is a full partner in the risks and a full partner in the rewards.

CUTTING WASTE AND RED TAPE

Dilbert is lucky he didn't have to travel for the Defense Department.

DILBERT reprinted by permission of United Feature Syndicate, Inc.

TALES FROM THE REINVENTION ZONE

Treating Travelers Like Honest People
Reform at the Defense Department is saving taxpayers $400 million a year.

Not too long ago, the Defense Department's travel process was like a bad dream. With 230 pages of travel regulations and multiple "sign-off" signatures, the 7 million trips that Defense Department travelers took were paper nightmares. The cost of Defense's travel system administration was triple that of private-sector corporations.

But that's all changing. The Department of Defense will soon have a travel system that will be the model for corporate travel management. The 230 pages of regulations have been reduced to 17 pages of plain English. Once the new system is in place, it will be completely paperless — and it will save more than $400 million annually, about two-thirds of the current cost of administration.

"We want to ride the travel industry's bow wave, not steer the ship," says Colonel Al Arnold, Project Manager of the Defense Travel System. Defense decided to partner with industry, using the best it had to offer. Now AT&T, American Express, EDS Corp., IBM, Carlson Wagonlit Travel, and a host of other large and small travel and information technology companies are sharing their best practices with Defense.

> **AT&T, American Express, EDS Corp., IBM, and Carlson Wagonlit Travel are sharing their best practices with Defense.**

Just like in industry, two basic principles have guided the Defense Department's efforts — government travelers are honest, and their supervisors are responsible but busy people. Instead of wading through travel regulations, they can use software that pops up "policy exceptions" for approval. The whole system has been reengineered from the moment travelers decide to go somewhere until they come back. Even the reimbursement of travelers' expenses is electronic — right to their bank accounts or to their charge card vendor.

The Defense Department will contract with one or a team of companies to provide the "how" of its new travel system. It has told the private sector what its performance requirements are, and now the private sector will tell Defense how to accomplish it. And the Defense Department has introduced a new idea — digital signatures on computerized travel forms. People won't even have to pick up a pen.

> *"DOD's travel reengineering has encouraged the integration of commercial products, which has required industry to partner in new and unique ways."*
>
> **David Hadsell**
> Director of Business Development, EDS

Citicorp and Country Homes

Citicorp has taught the U.S. Department of Agriculture (USDA) how to run a big-volume home mortgage operation.

USDA's Rural Development team has helped some 700,000 low-income families purchase homes. USDA's $18 billion portfolio is made up of home loans to families who cannot obtain mortgages from commercial banks. Until 1992, this vast program was administered at 2,000 field offices around the country, using a cumbersome system of card files and typewritten forms.

USDA asked for help from Citicorp, one of the country's largest commercial mortgage companies. "They asked if they could send a team to learn how we service mortgages," says Kim Gentile, former Assistant Vice President of Customer Service at Citicorp. "We liked the idea. They sent four USDA accountants to Citicorp for three months, where they helped to flow-chart our organization. It was a win-win situation. We received the flow charts, and they learned a lot about how to manage volume."

USDA learned how the day-to-day process of centralized loan servicing worked in the private sector and also what kind of equipment was available in a

> "USDA asked if they could send a team to learn how we service mortgages. We liked the idea."
>
> **Kim Gentile**
> Former Assistant VP of Customer Service, Citicorp

> **USDA's Rural Development Division has consolidated its loan servicing activities from 2,000 field offices into one central unit.**

centralized environment. In 1993, USDA set up a team of 25 employees who began to centralize and automate USDA's Rural Development process, modeling the new design on Citicorp.

Gentile left Citicorp to help reinvent the USDA program, so she has a unique perspective on the public and private sectors. "There is no question that there are excellent people in both the government and the private mortgage companies," she says. "Employees at Rural Development work extremely hard, and they really try to help the low-income families who are our customers. However, until recently this program just lacked the equipment and know-how to be able to manage its volume efficiently. The partnership between USDA and Citicorp helped the government employees acquire this know-how."

The results are an impressive victory over red tape. USDA's Rural Development Division has consolidated its loan servicing activities from 2,000 field offices into one central unit in St. Louis, and has cut out or consolidated 90 percent of the regulations on federal rural housing. The new loan system processes applications faster, and overall, USDA will cut the cost of servicing the portfolio by $250 million over five years.

Cutting to the Point

The Securities and Exchange Commission is getting companies to write prospectuses in language that is easy for the investor to understand.

Poor use of the English language leads to confusion, duplication, and error. Many businesses are discovering the benefits of writing in plain English. Ford Motor Company saw its leasing business skyrocket after it rewrote its lease documents so people could understand them.

A key principle of reinvention is to rewrite all complicated government information into plain English. The Securities and Exchange Commission is one of a number of federal agencies that is trying to do this by putting its own regulations in clear language. SEC is also working with companies to help them write their prospectuses and other disclosure documents in plain English. Anyone who has ever tried to read the fine print in these documents will see that this reform is long overdue.

Arthur Levitt, Chairman of the SEC, has spearheaded the effort. "Even with a lifetime of work in the securities industry, I can't understand some of these prospectuses, so how can anyone else? People put their life savings into these securities. There is no reason why companies shouldn't use everyday

> "Even with a lifetime of work in the securities industry, I can't understand some of these prospectuses."
>
> **Arthur Levitt**
> Chairman, SEC

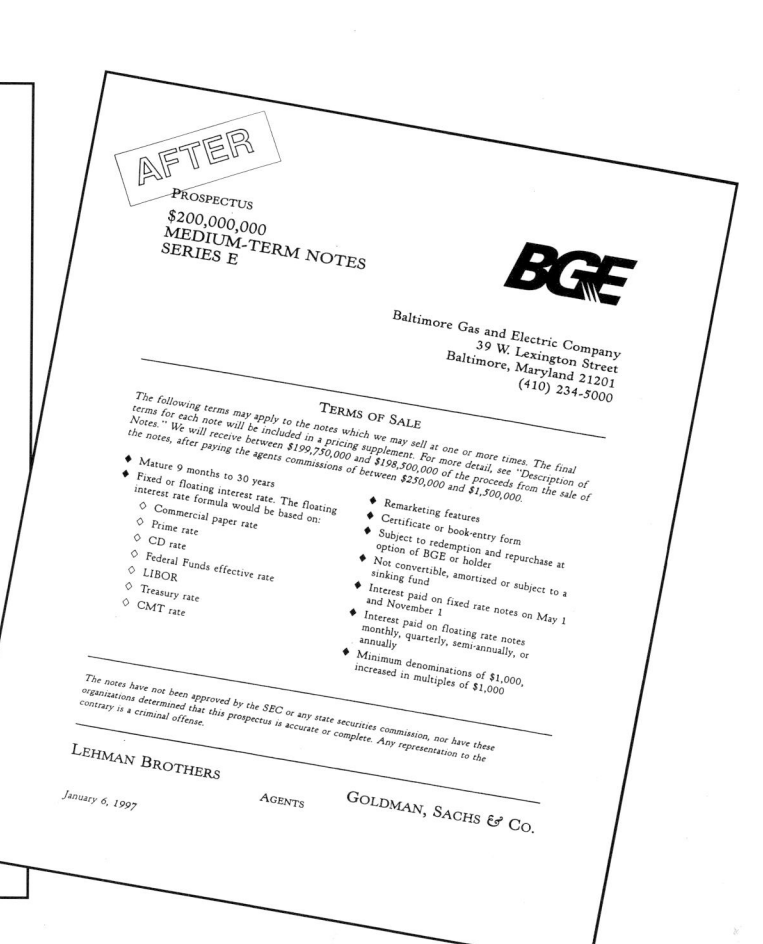

language so that the ordinary person — myself included — can understand what we're buying."

At Levitt's request, several companies volunteered to develop a new way of writing up the information. Bell Atlantic/NYNEX wrote the first prototype of a plain English prospectus. Others, like Baltimore Gas and Electric, followed.

Together, the SEC and business have come up with a new way of communicating financial information. There is now a handbook to help companies write clearly, located on the World Wide Web at *http://www.sec.gov/consumer/plaine.htm.* The SEC will shortly begin requiring that *all* prospectuses use plain English in the cover page, summary, and description of risk factors.

There is now a handbook on the Worldwide Web to help companies write clearly.

CHAPTER 5
Scream Savers
Technology is saving taxpayers time and money

Vacuum Tubes and Carbon Paper

Government is a latecomer to the information revolution. While corporate employees were using the latest high-tech tools, government employees were still using carbon paper. Because of complicated procurement procedures, even the computers government uses are often obsolete. The Federal Aviation Administration (FAA), for example, is still struggling to control air traffic with 30-year-old equipment dependent upon vacuum tubes.

Things got so bad that Congress passed a law exempting FAA from all the procurement rules. This is allowing FAA to work with industry to replace this obsolete air traffic control equipment with new video displays and computers.

It's been a different story in industry. Business discovered early on that access to information allows employees to work smarter. This has contributed to an enormous increase in innovation, productivity, and energy in corporations worldwide. Business has been able to reach new customers and markets and to

Making Information Technology Pay

develop a whole generation of new products — products that are customized to individual needs and delivered electronically.

The potential payoff from information technology is huge, but not automatic. The private sector has made effective use of technology by following three principles:

- *Don't automate the old process; reengineer.* The new technologies bring on new possibilities, like putting services on the World Wide Web and letting customers get them when they want.

- *Buy a little, test a little, fix a little.* A key difference between federal and private-sector information technology purchases is that the private sector buys things more quickly and in more manageable units.

Government often tries to buy huge systems. These systems take so long to acquire that the technology and the managers have both changed before anything is delivered.

SCREAM SAVERS

DILBERT reprinted by permission of United Feature Syndicate, Inc.

- *Buy commercial.* Commercial products and services provide wide variety and capability, and new ones are added every day. It almost always makes sense to sacrifice the "bells and whistles" to buy something that costs less and has been thoroughly tested.

Don't automate the old process; reengineer.

REINVENTION ZONE INTERVIEW

Swiping Stamps

Consider the case of Jack Radzikowski, head of the Federal Financial Systems Branch, Office of Management and Budget (OMB), and former director of the Vice President's EBT Task Force. He has unleashed information technology to save money and cut fraud in the food stamp program.

Q. How does the food stamp program work?

A. About 9.5 million households receive food stamps totaling $24 billion per year. The federal government prints this "private money" and ships it under armed guard to regional centers. Then it goes to the states, and they distribute it to families. After use, it has to be collected, counted and re-counted, and finally burned. All this costs over $70 million a year.

There's also fraud. Coupon books are sold on the street for half of their face value, and sometimes that money is used to buy illegal drugs.

Otherwise, food stamps work great.

SCREAM SAVERS

Q. What does the Electronic Benefits Transfer (EBT) program change?

A. Just about everything. Eligible households receive an EBT card. It looks like a credit card. The EBT card is "swiped" through the same point of service (POS) machine at the food store that takes credit and debit cards. The whole transaction is recorded instantaneously. There is limited potential for fraud.

Q. How did the EBT revolution begin?

A. First, the private sector and states created an EBT Council composed of the major stakeholders in the POS system: the banking system, the state benefits people, and the grocery store associations. They helped make the key decision — the EBT system would be compatible with private-sector POS standards.

Then, individual states or multi-state "buying clubs" put EBT contracts out for bid to banking and other transaction systems. The "buying clubs" share services, creating higher volumes to drive down costs.

Q. And now?

A. In the summer of 1997, seven states have fully operational EBT systems. Fifteen more states have partial systems, and all the rest are in the process of acquiring a card issuer. Our goal is to cut costs and reduce fraud. We expect to have all the states on EBT by the end of 1999.

> *Our goal is to cut costs and reduce fraud.*

Electronic transactions are now encouraged everywhere.

Panel 1: I CANNOT ALLOW THIS WITHDRAWAL... (BANK OF ETHEL)
Panel 2: UNLESS YOU DEFEAT ME IN HAND TO HAND COMBAT.
Panel 3: THEY SEEM PRETTY SERIOUS ABOUT ENCOURAGING THE USE OF THEIR AUTOMATED TELLER MACHINES.

DILBERT reprinted by permission of United Feature Syndicate, Inc.

Q. What about food stores without POS?

A. We are convinced that if food stamp program recipients use only EBT cards, then stores who want their business will get wired for POS. So EBT is encouraging the "wiring of America." By the way, EBT users will look like any other consumer using a card at a POS machine. That is an enormous plus.

Q. What are your cost data so far?

A. Monthly costs per EBT card user are hovering around $1 versus $3 to $4 in the food stamp system. If more benefit programs are provided on EBT cards — like social security, veterans, railroad retirement, and state benefit programs — we could save somewhere between $200 million and a quarter billion dollars a year, every year. And at last state and federal benefit programs will be able to monitor cash flow on a daily basis and track where their dollars are going.

In addition, the EBT card might serve as an account for indigent people without a bank, providing a safe way to receive funds and benefits.

Q. Is EBT a federal system?

A. EBT is not a federal system. The federal government sends the benefit dollars electronically to the states, and that's about it. The states contract with a card issuer who designs and distributes the EBT card. In addition, the states decide what other benefits it will provide in addition to food stamps.

Q. Any final comments?

A. Just one. I want to thank the private sector for designing such a wonderful, cost-effective public-sector benefits distribution system. I'm only partly kidding. They were smart enough to design the optimum transaction system in the heat of the marketplace. We were smart enough to see POS could provide something beyond credit or debit services. We were both smart enough to see that we could and should work together in partnership.

> *We could save somewhere between $200 million and a quarter billion dollars a year.*

TALES FROM THE REINVENTION ZONE

Beating Computer Swords into Corporate Shares
Sandia National Laboratories in Albuquerque has partnered with Goodyear to design safer tires.

Sandia National Laboratories, a part of the Department of Energy, designs and tests nuclear weapons using a computer. Obviously, that takes a world-class computer. Sandia's computer is 300 times faster than IBM's "Deep Blue," the chess champion.

Goodyear is the only remaining U.S.-owned original equipment tire manufacturer. In 1992, Loren Miller, Goodyear's director of performance modeling, read a Sandia research paper on computer modeling. Intrigued, he called Sandia.

Miller was astonished. "Sandia's computer can model all kinds of conditions for nuclear weapons — rain, heat, freezing, collisions, and so on. These same things happen to tires. In fact, modeling tire performance is one of the most challenging problems in computational physics. We got together, and Sandia found the job tough enough to be interesting."

Having proved "tough enough," Goodyear began collaborating with Sandia. "Sandia-based models have changed the way we design and test. Tires perform on the test track exactly as the computer predicted. This could really reduce the time and money required to design and test tires," says Miller.

"Sandia has started similar research partnerships with other corporations for a total of $42 million in 1997, and we hope to exceed $100 million by 2000," says Dan Hartley, Sandia's Vice President for Partnership. Other Department of Energy labs, including Los Alamos, are also applying their highly sophisticated computer and engineering skills in joint research projects with the private sector.

www.business.gov

Businesses can now obtain most government information from a single source.

Business helpline

A common complaint about government is that people have to go door to door to door for the information they need. For business the problem was acute: 40 different agencies regulate or provide services to business. The Small Business Administration, with the help of a number of agencies, came up with a solution.

Business now has a new one-stop electronic department store: the U.S. Business Advisor at *www.business.gov* on

> **The site answers questions on payroll, taxes, exports, and employment.**

the World Wide Web. Originally shown by President Clinton at the White House Conference on Small Business in 1995, this product was designed and redesigned based on reactions from business people who tried it. They loved the idea of one electronic stop, but wanted to change just about everything else. So we did.

The new advisor, released this spring, lets businesses search 106,000 federal World Wide Web addresses for information by typing in simple English questions. The advisor answers in seconds with key passages highlighted.

The site provides answers to commonly asked questions on topics including payroll, taxes, exports, labor, employment, business software, benefits, and venture capital. It offers the capacity to download most forms related to business. It also links the user to specific federal agency home pages. For example, the Small Business Administration put its fast-track loan applications online to be filled out and submitted electronically.

The U.S. Business Advisor levels the playing field by giving small firms the same access to government information and contracts as a major corporation with its large resources. It is an invaluable time- and cost-saving tool for all companies.

SCREAM SAVERS

Over 400,000 companies used the service in its first two months of operation. Eighty-nine percent said the U.S. Business Advisor "makes it easier for us to do business with the government."

Online, Not In Line

There is finally an easy way to find federal statistics — without having to know in advance which department produces the data.

FedStats is another window into the federal government — in this case into the wealth of statistical information the government collects. The Web site (*www.fedstats.gov*) uses the Internet's powerful link and search capabilities to bring users information from some 70 federal agencies.

The service features an A-to-Z index, a keyword search capability, and a "Fastfacts" link, as well as a host of data listed by topic, region, program, and department. It also links up to sources of international statistics.

Sally Katzen, head of the Office of Information and Regulatory Affairs, described FedStats' significance this way: "Today a high school student in Boise, Idaho, has better access to federal statistics than top officials in Washington had five years ago."

> **A high school student in Boise has easy access to federal statistics.**

Miracles at MEDLINE

The National Institutes of Health (NIH) free MEDLINE service — http://www.nlm.nih.gov/databases/freemedl.html — is invaluable to physicians and patients.

In June 1997, Vice President Gore announced free online access to the NIH/National Library of Medicine's MEDLINE, the world's largest source of published medical information. Previously, users had to register and pay to search these important online research archives.

Even when it was a for-fee service, MEDLINE created miracles:

- A Maryland woman who'd had several miscarriages consulted MEDLINE, found a treatment, and carried a baby successfully to term.

- A Virginia couple's six-month search of medical literature resulted in treatment for their son's rare inherited disease — a search that became famous in the movie *Lorenzo's Oil*.

A free MEDLINE is particularly valuable to smaller companies that previously had to limit their searches due to cost. They can now conduct wide-ranging medical literature searches, producing more innovation faster and at lower cost. But most of all, a free MEDLINE enables individual citizens to take charge of their health.

SCREAM SAVERS

Look For Medicare Under "H"
The General Services Administration is bringing common sense to the phone directory.

Americans turn to the blue pages 81 million times a year to look up a phone number for the federal government. Half the time they find it; the other half they give up in frustration. After all, who would guess that Medicare is listed under "H" — for Department of Health and Human Services?

Working in partnership with Ameritech, Bell Atlantic, Pacific Telephone, and Sprint, the General Services Administration is making the blue pages more sensible. This consortium has already revamped the blue pages that serve 111 million Americans, with the rest to be fixed in the next year. The new blue pages are modeled after the yellow pages. They are arranged by service, not by organization, in big type and cross-referenced with fax numbers and Internet addresses.

The new government blue pages are modeled after the yellow pages.

No Inventory—Just Like Home Depot
Patients get fresher supplies faster.

Health supplies— just-in-time

When the Departments of Defense and Veterans Affairs wanted to streamline their practices for distributing pharmaceuticals and medical supplies, they didn't attempt to automate old process. They sent their managers to look at the commercial health care industry. They got an eyeful.

The health care industry used a just-in-time distribution system. It contracted with manufacturers and wholesale distributors to deliver products on demand. By contrast, the government had medical depots spread across the country. Central buyers ordered supplies for the depots, then a costly delivery system shipped stock to the users. Government workers hustled to make sure the oldest inventory was shipped — unless its shelf life had run out, in which case they threw it out and shipped the newer stock.

Defense and VA both reengineered. They got rid of most of the depot system, replacing it with contracts that guarantee one-day delivery of medical items through local distributors, at government (i.e., *low*) prices. Hospitals order direct from the vendors electronically — just like Home Depot does.

At Defense alone, inventory has been slashed, and costs have been cut by $680 million. Customer service has improved as well, with 166,000 items available compared to 15,000 in the old depot system.

"Our traditional system was too slow and too expensive. We took most of what we had learned about logistics over the past 20 years and threw it out the window. Then we did what made good business sense for our customers — relied on the U.S. industrial base," says Sally Bird, Deputy Director, Medical Materiel, Defense Personnel Support Center.

Says Milt Minor, National Director of Government Services, McKesson Health Systems, "This is a government/industry partnership that has helped Defense control health care costs while enhancing health care quality. It has assisted the military in redeploying its assets while improving its ability to respond to its patients' needs at a lower cost to the government."

> "We did what made good business sense for our customers — relied on the U.S. industrial base."
>
> **Sally Bird**
> Defense Personnel Support Center

Technology: Bite-sized
The "small is beautiful" philosophy will save taxpayers $1.8 billion.

Defense is replacing 79 procurement systems with one commercial software product.

In the past, when government needed new large information systems, it would spend years writing specifications and then contract for years of technology development. It was common for this process to cost billions of dollars. And in the end, agencies often ended up with hugely dysfunctional systems, or nothing at all. Finally the government is adopting the buy-a-little, test-a-little, fix-a-little approach.

The Defense Department has 48,000 buyers who handle procurement from 950 different sites. These buyers used to have 79 separate procurement information systems. Now Defense is replacing those systems with one commercial software product from American Management Systems (AMS) that runs on commercial PCs. The software is being tested at 100 sites. Based on the feedback gained from this first test, AMS will customize the software as needed. After a similar test at 300 more sites, AMS will tweak again and create the final version. Four years from now, all Defense buyers will be on one system, saving Defense some $1.8 billion in the next eight years.

SCREAM SAVERS

Call London for 7 Cents a Minute
The government is saving money by buying telecommunication services commercially.

The General Services Administration is leveraging the buying power of the whole government to get its customer agencies the world's best prices for commercially available tele-communication services. On domestic long-distance voice calls the government is now paying 1.9 cents to 5.5 cents per minute — 11.6 percent below the lowest commercial equivalent.

And GSA has broken new ground in buying international services, wireless services, and high-speed data services. For example, international long-distance calls to the United Kingdom have been cut from 30 cents a minute to 7 cents. GSA has negotiated commercial wireless rates 20 to 60 percent below best commercial rates, and for the first time has made service available anywhere in the country.

Businesses now can meet more government needs through their commercial offerings. Donald E. Scott of GTE Government Systems Corporation puts it this way: "The government is using its buying power and has stepped back from requiring unique features, which lets us do what we do best — deliver commercial service."

> **The government is using its buying power to get the world's best telephone prices.**

BUSINESSLIKE GOVERNMENT

CHAPTER 6

Do the Right Thing
Regulators are more effective in partnership with industry

Good or Evil?

To many Americans in regulated industries, it must have seemed that government thought they were evil.

Consider this quote from a manual for federal regulators: "All regulatory processes are designed to discover and develop evidence of violations."

Far too often, regulatory agencies focused only on finding violators, rather than preventing problems. This attitude was reinforced by the incentive system. "Success" in the regulatory world meant finding the most violations and issuing the highest fines. Government told business exactly what to do, and how to do it — all specified in thousands of detailed, often incomprehensible rules and regulations. Then regulatory agencies spent their time trying to catch companies when they made a mistake. One agency even referred to those it monitored as "suspects."

These federal regulatory systems were merely a reflection of the times. American society was organized around top-down, command-and-control models. It had worked well for Henry Ford, after all. And in many ways it had worked well for regulators. Strong enforcement woke business up. The air is cleaner than it was before

Partnership Works Best

the Environmental Protection Agency (EPA) came on the scene, and workers are safer since the Occupational Health and Safety Administration (OSHA) opened in the 1970s. Smart employers now accept that they have a responsibility to keep the environment clean, to keep their workers safe, and to produce safe and healthy products.

For employers that accept these responsibilities, the role of regulators is changing. The best way to protect the public is by *preventing* violations, not just punishing them. Regulators can help industry achieve compliance through training and education, by sharing best practices, and by developing consensual approaches and encouraging innovation. Regulators need to work in partnership with industry and communities to design regulatory processes to get clean air and water, healthy food, and safe workers.

And working *with* good players allows regulatory agencies to put more people to work catching those who *do* intentionally violate and disregard the law.

Companies know their own business. They often have the best ideas for solving problems. Many are willing to help government develop new regulatory approaches that leverage their corporate intelligence and resources and require them to take responsibility and be held accountable.

DO THE RIGHT THING

When government works in partnership with its stakeholders, everybody wins. Stakeholders include business, labor, communities, non-governmental organizations, and individuals. When regulators focus on what really matters — prevention, not punishment — business can do business, customers are better served, and regulators get the results they seek. That's much more than can be achieved under a strictly command-and-control approach.

In case after case, regulatory agencies are discovering they can do better with partnerships than without them. Seventy percent of companies that formed a partnership with OSHA in the Maine 200 program saw worker illness and injury rates drop substantially. The partnership between the Coast Guard and the towing and barge industry is so effective that, without a single new regulation, crew fatalities have dropped by half. When EPA challenged industry in its 33/50 program to commit voluntarily to reduced emissions, 750 million pounds of toxic chemicals were kept out of our environment. By working with the pharmaceutical industry, the Food and Drug Administration (FDA) has improved public health by reducing the time to approve safe and effective drugs from 23 months to 15.

So partnership can work — the results speak for themselves.

Cooperation Pays Off

70% of companies that formed a partnership with OSHA saw worker illness and injury rates drop.

REINVENTION ZONE INTERVIEW

Mile-High Partnership

Consider the case of Wendell Gardner, Senior Vice President at COBE, a Denver-based manufacturer of medical devices. Gardner — while leading an FDA/industry task force — has seen regulatory reinvention work first-hand.

Q. What does your company make?

A. We manufacture what the FDA calls medical devices — in our case, kidney dialysis machines, heart-lung machines, and transfusion machines that harvest and separate blood components.

Q. What's it like dealing with the FDA?

A. It's a lot better than it used to be.

Q. How so?

A. We used to have a very adversarial relationship on both sides, because we didn't have common objectives. FDA thought the industry was out to rip off the public and didn't really care about quality. And industry viewed the government as being against innovation.

Q. What sort of things went on?

A. Since we didn't have a common objective, the FDA's position was, "It's not our job to help you, it's our job to nail you." They would come out to a plant and just be on a witch hunt. They'd hang out and look and look and look until they could find something wrong.

They inspected paperwork instead of the product. You could have virtually a perfect product in the field, and the FDA would give you a violation like this: "You said you would inspect 1 out of 10 devices, and write down the serial number, the date, the time, and the name and initials of the inspector. We checked 100 of the records and found 5 without initials. Therefore you have an adulterated product in the field."

And the law included criminal penalties for violations. The FDA came to our plant, gave us a list of violations, and then sent me a letter saying I should show cause why I shouldn't be indicted. When I showed up at the hearing, the regional compliance officer who had sent me the letter was sitting as judge and jury, too. I just about left the industry over that.

> **Industry and the FDA started a grass-roots partnership that has made some real improvements.**

Q. But we need a sure way to protect the public, don't we?

A. Of course, and there will always be some bad apples that you have to get tough with. But for most of the industry, the regulators shouldn't be adversaries. Let me give you an example. COBE sells products overseas. Our relationship with the international bodies that regulate us has always been much less adversarial. For instance, they call ahead to schedule their visits. As a result, their visits are more productive, and the international public is still well-protected.

Q. But now things are getting better stateside?

A. Right. Industry and the FDA started a grass-roots partnership that has made some real improvements.

Q. Like what?

A. It used to be that every inspection was a surprise. Now, they let companies know when they're scheduled for routine inspections. That way, we can have the people and records they need on hand. The FDA investigators themselves say it takes less time and doesn't compromise quality.

And they used to keep everything a secret from us until the end of the inspection, then write us a formal letter. Now, during the inspection, they let companies know what they think we are doing wrong. That gives us a chance to correct any misperceptions they might have and to fix some of the real problems on the spot.

Q. Are you happy now?
A. We still have things to work on, like the product approval process, the criteria for warning letters, and the continuing evaluation of inspections.

But we're going to be able to solve these problems because FDA and industry now have common objectives: Better patient outcomes and a strong U.S.-based medical device industry. And we are working through the grass-roots partnership to achieve those objectives.

Now, during inspections, we can fix some of the real problems on the spot.

TALES FROM THE REINVENTION ZONE

Miami Virtue

In Miami, the trade community and three federal agencies are working together to clear cargo faster and intercept more drugs.

In Miami, the three agencies most involved with the flow of international commerce — Customs, Immigration and Naturalization Service, and USDA — streamlined their business procedures to improve service to business and travelers.

"Everyone was frustrated when I first got here," says Lynn Gordon, the director of Customs in Miami. "Historically, Customs had focused on enforcement, and as a result we were delaying, damaging, or seizing lots of cargo and writing lots of tickets. Business owners didn't like paying violations; we didn't like processing them." Meanwhile, legitimate cargo was held up from entering U.S. commerce. Imported flowers were left for days to wilt on the tarmac. And international passengers were kept waiting in the terminal for up to three hours.

"What I really wanted was compliance, not penalties," Gordon said. She made it her job to talk to the trade community: "I spent countless hours meeting with industry and airport representatives to talk about

DO THE RIGHT THING

their business needs and the frustration caused by regulatory red tape.

Business leaders told me something they'd been trying to tell us for years. They said: 'Every time we see you it's because there's a problem, and the conversation is always unpleasant. If you would just talk to us and tell us what you want, we'll do it. Don't keep us in the dark, then show up unexpectedly and try to catch us in the wrong. *Help us help you*. And by the way, we've got some ideas about how to be helpful.' "

So Gordon revamped the way Miami Customs did its work. She formed a partnership with the trade community and with the Immigration and Naturalization Service and USDA to work on mutual goals, like promoting legitimate trade and stopping drug shipments. Customs held weekly seminars for the business community on how to comply with federal requirements and succeed in international trade. By pooling resources and using information technology, Customs and its partners could target their interdiction efforts toward the small percentage of shipments and passengers that were in violation of federal laws. As a result, legitimate cargo was cleared quickly, drug seizures doubled, and international passengers' waiting time dropped to as little as 20 minutes.

> *"What I really wanted was compliance, not penalties."*
>
> **Lynn Gordon**
> Miami Customs

This approach led the way for other innovations as well. Companies that used to file a form for every import/export transaction (which in one case resulted in one company filing 700,000 forms in a single year) now file one consolidated form per month. Gordon learned about the 700,000 forms at a local business meeting. "You don't find out about this stuff if you don't get out and talk to people."

Gordon's approach has been a raging success, and members of the Miami business community are her biggest fans. But she also has fans sprinkled throughout the federal government — regulators from other agencies who were also tired of the fighting and knew there must be a better way. OSHA, among others, has sent its own regulators down to Miami to learn from Gordon's team. And her model is being replicated.

> **Companies that used to file a form for every import/export transaction now file one consolidated form per month.**

DO THE RIGHT THING

[Dilbert comic strip]

DILBERT reprinted by permission of United Feature Syndicate, Inc.

Safety, Plain and Simple

OSHA provides expert workplace safety advice in plain English on the World Wide Web; no lawyers needed to interpret.

Most business people want to do what's right by keeping the environment clean and protecting their workers. Often, companies have to hire lawyers just to understand what the regulations require. The Occupational Safety and Health Administration heard the frustrations of the business community and responded in two ways. It began a plain English initiative, rewriting the rule book to make the regulations easy to understand. And it's established "expert advisors" on the Internet to answer important business questions.

If a small business contractor has a question about working with asbestos, for example, she can download

> "The Asbestos Advisor is a wonderful example of making the government more attuned to the needs of its clients, the regulated community."
>
> **Frank Livingston**
> Senior VP,
> Draper & Kramer, Inc.

OSHA's Asbestos Advisor at the public library, at home, or anywhere with Internet access. She can tell the advisor all the specific details of the job she's doing, and the advisor will give her safety information, permit requirements, and other sources of information, all free. The advisor might even tell her that she isn't covered by these requirements.

There are automated expert advisors on the same Web site that will answer questions about cadmium safety and working in confined spaces. Eventually, there will be advisors for additional topics. OSHA didn't develop these advisors in a vacuum, but invited representatives of interested trade associations, small businesses, and labor to comment on the early versions.

The advisors can be reached at *http://www.osha.gov/oshasoft*. And they are getting rave reviews. According to Frank Livingston, Senior Vice President of Draper & Kramer Inc., a property management company, "The Asbestos Advisor is a wonderful example of making the government more attuned to the needs of its clients, the regulated community."

Taken together, OSHA's plain English initiatives and the advisors allow businesses to focus on getting the job done, instead of spending time and legal fees trying to figure out just what the rules require them to do.

DO THE RIGHT THING

Bare Knuckles to Brass Tacks

EPA is applying business solutions to environmental issues — they work better and cost less. Sound familiar?

"The rivers had stopped burning — and that was good," said John DeVillars, Regional Administrator of the Environmental Protection Agency in New England. "The Cuyahoga River catching fire in 1969 in Cleveland was part of what we call the first generation of environmental issues — the alarming things that woke people up and gave the EPA such a strong regulatory mandate when it was created back in 1970."

When DeVillars was Secretary of Environmental Affairs in Massachusetts in the late 1980s, he was known as a bare-knuckle environmental enforcer. Then he spent several years working for Coopers and Lybrand and developed a broader perspective. As DeVillars describes it, "When I took this job in 1994, I recognized there was a need for a more standardized approach if we were to tackle the more complex and subtle second generation of environmental issues. Issues like particulate emission levels in the air and watershed protection. These issues aren't visible and frightening enough to get much public attention, but they have a huge impact on the quality of life in New England. To tackle this second generation effectively, EPA was going

> *"The rivers had stopped burning — and that was good."*
>
> **John DeVillars**
> EPA, New England

> **"We had to shift our focus from violations to increasing compliance."**
>
> **John DeVillars**
> EPA, New England

to have to undergo a major cultural shift. In addition to providing strong enforcement, we had to shift our focus from violations to increasing compliance."

It started with a major restructuring. Traditionally, EPA organized at the national and regional levels into "stovepipes" that didn't always relate well to one another — one division for water, one for air, etc. This was incredibly frustrating to industry. "One factory might find itself dealing with three or four different divisions and sets of rules just from our office," says DeVillars. So he based his reorganization, in part, on being easily accessible to industry, following the lead of EPA Administrator Carol Browner and her Common Sense Initiative. Now there are teams organized along industry lines: a printing team, a metal finishing team, an electronics team, and so on.

"That was the easy part. Then we started to privatize parts of our regulatory function, and things got really exciting," he says.

"We were finding that most businesses are in compliance with regulations, and that many of our enforcement efforts were pursuing marginal, low-risk infractions. And again, we weren't focused enough on resolving the second generation of risks. Issues like the danger we face from polluted indoor air or from

DO THE RIGHT THING

agricultural and storm-water runoff were getting too little attention."

DeVillars knew from his private-sector experience that business has long employed certified financial auditors to review companies' financial statements, and he reasoned that this approach could work for the EPA as well. DeVillars established StarTrack, designed to develop a class of certified, independent professionals who assess compliance with environmental laws. These environmental auditors are proving that independent professionals can monitor performance as well as or better than government inspectors — and at less cost to the taxpayers. At the same time, EPA has focused its enforcement efforts on the worst violators — and with positive results. Last year the regional office broke all records for prosecution of criminal violations.

William Sweetman, manager of Environmental Engineering at Spalding Sports Worldwide in Chicopee, Massachusetts, represents one of the companies volunteering to work with DeVillars. The group also includes Gillette, Texas Instruments, and International Paper. "The rigorous third-party environmental audit performed as part of the StarTrack program has allowed Spalding to recognize and realize valuable improvements in operation,"

> **From his private-sector experience, DeVillars knew that business uses certified financial auditors. He brought this approach to EPA.**

Sweetman explained. "The continued development of these tools will enhance the quality of Spalding's environmental program, while minimizing the federal and state resources needed to ensure Spalding's continued compliance on a permanent basis."

"In a few years," says DeVillars, "the public may be able to judge a company by reviewing two certified reports, one for financial performance and one for environmental performance. EPA will audit a percentage of the companies and the certifiers, to maintain the integrity of the system. At the same time, we will be able to redeploy lots of people from the general compliance monitoring to aggressive enforcement against dangerous violators. StarTrack lets everybody win — except the bad guys."

> "We will be able to redeploy lots of people from general compliance monitoring to aggressive enforcement against dangerous violators."
>
> **John DeVillars**
> EPA, New England

Speeding Relief

FDA is helping a small company get faster approval of replacement skin that speeds recovery and alleviates pain and suffering for burn victims.

Advanced Tissue Sciences (ATS), a small biotech company in southern California, makes things that not long ago were science fiction — like replacement skin for burn patients. These products are regulated by the Food and Drug Administration. Together their goal is to get these new products to the people who need them as quickly as possible.

"In the past there was an adversarial relationship between the FDA and the manufacturers — not much in the way of trust in either direction," recalls Doug Christian, ATS's Director of Quality Assurance. "I've worked for companies that were on the receiving end of that attitude and I've personally been stung by it. For example, in one company I worked for, FDA came out for a regularly scheduled inspection — there hadn't been any problems, just a routine inspection. But without letting us in on it, the FDA had raised the standard on software design. They just beat us up — it cost the company thousands. Overnight, we went from being good guys to bad guys, and we didn't even know what had happened."

"But there has been a 180-degree cultural shift in FDA," says Christian. "It can't be judged as anything less."

Gail Naughton, Ph.D., the President and Chief Operating Officer at ATS, says that FDA's new attitude will make it possible to put replacement skin on the market a full year earlier. "The difference between getting approval in 12 months rather than 24 months is huge," she says. "While you're waiting, you have to keep all of your people employed and keep your manufacturing area up, but you can't be producing product — or get it to the people who need it."

How is FDA moving so much faster? "The telephone is a breakthrough," says Naughton. "FDA used to mail formal, dated letters, and you couldn't respond until you actually had the letter in your hands. For them to call and say, 'Let's get together tomorrow at 9:30 and hash this out,' saves weeks every time. They don't even bother with formal letters anymore, they send informal faxes. They work the East Coast-West Coast time very well. They work late in Washington to fax us questions before we go home, so we can get them the answers overnight and call them back first thing in the morning. Sometimes we call Sunday night to leave them a voice mail, and they pick up the phone. Most large businesses don't work that effectively."

> "There has been a 180-degree cultural shift in FDA."
>
> **Doug Christian**
> Director of Quality Assurance, ATS

DO THE RIGHT THING

> **"The more uncertainty you can cut out of the process, the more capital will flow into the biotech industry."**
>
> **Art Benvenuto**
> Chairman and CEO, ATS

Another big change: FDA improved the review process. "They brought in clinicians who understand clinical design and specialists in bioengineering. Now that experts review us, we don't have to spend all our time educating them. We used to have to explain everything."

"Consistency also helps get these kinds of products to market," says ATS's Chairman and CEO, Art Benvenuto. "FDA decided who would review us and stuck to that decision," he says. "That took the ambiguity out of the process, which is important in raising the capital for innovative product development. The more uncertainty you can cut out of the process, the more capital will flow into the biotech industry, which provides the jobs and, most importantly, the high-quality products that Americans need. This should be a model for other regulatory agencies."

In coming years, many patients will benefit from the new approach. "Our next product coming to clinical trials is cartilage, to repair joints like knees and shoulders damaged in auto accidents or sports," reports Naughton. "The old FDA would never tell you in advance how to structure your testing or what data they wanted. They'd only tell you afterwards that what you had done wasn't good enough. Now we are talking with them way up front. That way, we can do the tests right the first time."

FDA's new approach is helping patients worldwide. "FDA has set the trend by expediting the process. Now Canada, South Africa, and Australia are moving faster too."

"You just get tired of hearing people say negative things about government all the time," says Naughton. "It's not like we've had just one good experience. We've been working smoothly together for nearly three years now."

Gut Issues
Protecting our food supply from ever-changing microbes is a continuing challenge for regulators and business.

You are what you eat

As our understanding of foodborne illness expands, we identify new risks. The recent recall of 25 million pounds of ground beef due to possible contamination with E. coli bacteria points out the need for business and government to work together to develop new approaches — and to leverage resources — to ensure food safety.

In 1993, the E. coli strain O157:H7 killed several children who ate tainted hamburgers, and in 1996 it caused the recall of a particular brand of unpasteurized apple cider. Since 1996, E. coli has evolved into newer strains that create additional threats. To cope with both the known and the unknown threats, the U.S. Department of

DO THE RIGHT THING

> "Inspections will never catch more than a fraction of tainted food. That's why every effort must be made to prevent contamination during production."
>
> **Business Week**

Agriculture developed a package-labeling program that warns consumers to fully cook beef and chicken in order to destroy any pathogens present.

Increased understanding of E. coli and other food-borne pathogens, the expansion of international trade in food, and the growing diversity of our food systems and sources has led to a general recognition that new approaches are necessary. Historically, inspection of food products occurred at the endpoint of the process and was the responsibility of a woefully understaffed federal inspection force. As *Business Week* said in a recent editorial: "Inspections will never catch more than a fraction of tainted food. That's why every effort must be made to prevent contamination during production."

In partnership with industry and consumer groups, the federal government has developed a new approach called HACCP, which stands for Hazard Analysis and Critical Control Points. This approach builds prevention into food production systems and requires food producers to self-inspect — taking day-to-day responsibility for food quality.

To meet the food safety challenge, flexible strategies are being developed that allow for tailored approaches to specific problems; both industry and government are adopting better inspection and detection methods; and public information campaigns are spreading the word about proper food preparation and kitchen cleanliness.

Partnership and shared responsibility can fix many of the problems. However, it is an essential role of government to police the marketplace. In food safety as in other areas of federal regulatory responsibility, strong enforcement must remain an option. There will always be times when, as in the ground beef case, the government has to step in and take strong action.

CHAPTER 7

Show me the Reinvention!
Believe that government has been reinvented when you see it

Who hasn't heard that movie line "Show me the money"? But that attitude is not unique to sports contracts; most people care more for results than for promises. That goes for "better government," as well.

I can state with complete confidence that government is better today than when we started this effort four years ago. We have found groups of workers all across government, many of them in what we designated "reinvention labs," who have been experimenting with new ways. We have spotlighted and praised the most successful experiments — started hundreds of fires of change and fanned the flames. Now some bonfires are raging, ready to sweep entire agencies, starting with the ones that affect the public and business most.

> **The FDA will cut review time for new medical devices by 30 percent.**

By the year 2000, you will notice a difference in those agencies. For example:

- If you are a student (or the parent of one), you'll be able to apply for college financial aid over the Internet and find out your aid eligibility within four days, cutting in half the current processing time. The forms will be simple; the instructions will be in plain English; and if you call with a question you'll get a quick, courteous answer. Faster aid decisions will reduce the anxiety at a tough time for students and parents and give them more time to make the right choices in picking the right college.

- The Food and Drug Administration will cut review time for important new medical devices by 30 percent, speed drug approvals, provide you with better information on medical products, and assure improved quality of your food.

- The Weather Service will be giving you twice as much warning of severe weather; that means you'll have a better chance of finding safe shelter.

And within the next decade, the Federal Aviation Administration will reduce city-to-city flight delays and, with some help from NASA and the Defense Department, cut the aircraft accident rate by 80 percent.

SHOW ME THE REINVENTION!

For space flights, NASA will slash the cost per pound of rocket payloads, and the agency will get more of its scientific discoveries to teachers and students fast.

These are just a few examples of how government will answer the "show me the reinvention" challenge. They are drawn from goals set by the agencies as concrete promises of action — promises they will keep. The agencies are committed to report their progress to the public. That is common practice in business; it is called a report to stockholders. Now that kind of report will be common practice in government as well.

But setting goals and reporting progress is not enough. There is no one simple fix. It will take the efforts of people in government, people in business, and individual citizens to make government work better and cost less.

This book emphasized what government has learned from business. We can't say often enough how much we appreciate the willingness of the business community to share lessons. Some of the best examples of reinvented government, in fact, are the result of ongoing partnerships with high-performing private-sector companies.

> **Some of the best examples of reinvented government are the result of ongoing partnerships with high-performing companies.**

We took the lessons learned from the successful reinventors — both in and out of government — and distilled them into a set of "rules of the road." President Clinton's cabinet learned about these rules at a retreat at Blair House in Washington before the January 1997 inauguration. We put these lessons into a book called *The Blair House Papers*, and this book is now near the top of the government best-seller list.

Here is one indicator that we are on the right track: Public trust in the federal government has improved by 9 percentage points over the past four years, reversing a 30-year decline.

There is still much more to be done, but by collaborating with businesses that want their government to succeed, we'll get there. Restoring the faith of Americans in their government will be tough. The only way agencies can make this happen is by convincing their customers, one by one, that things have changed.

> **Public trust in the federal government has improved by 9 percentage points over the past 4 years.**

My vision is that when John or Jane Q. Public deals with the government — Social Security, the IRS, or any other federal agency — afterwards they will say, "I expected a hard time — but that was easy." Or, "Some department stores can be really helpful, but this agency was even better."

When that happens, it will show them the reinvention. When that happens, we will have reinvented a government that works better and costs less. When that happens, the faith of Americans in their government will be restored.

Al Gore

Al Gore

Acknowledgments

The story of reinventing government is first and foremost the story of 1,900,000 public servants striving, reaching, struggling to serve America. No large institution in America has a more dedicated or more competent workforce. For four years we have been telling the story of how they are making government work better and cost less, starting with the first report of the National Performance Review in 1993. We're grateful to all of them.

Once again this year, stories of their successes have flowed in from dozens of agencies and from the individuals, businesses, and governments they serve. We regret that we could not use all of these success stories — we had a tough time choosing.

This year's report focuses on an unheralded success: the way government is learning from the most successful American businesses. Dozens of companies furthered the reinvention effort by sharing their successful practices and working with us to implement them in the federal government. The report highlights the achievements of these companies that have been emulated in the federal workplace, but of course, their inclusion here does not constitute a general endorsement of the companies by either the National Performance Review or by Vice President Al Gore.

Index

Abbe, Paul O., Inc.	17-19
Adams, Scott	4
Advanced Tissue Sciences (ATS)	95-98
Agency for International Development, US (USAID)	33-35
Agriculture, Department of (USDA)	56-57, 86-88, 98-99
Rural Development	56-57
Albuquerque	68
Allford, Suzanne	25
American Express	54
Travel Related Services	21
American Management Systems (AMS)	76
Ameritech	73
Archuleta, Phil	38-39
Army	48
Arnold, Al	54
AT&T	22, 36, 37, 54
Universal Card Services	21
Baltimore Gas and Electric	59
Banc One	25
Beals, Vaughn	28
Bell Atlantic/NYNEX	59, 73
Bell Canada	21
Benvenuto, Art	97
Bird, Sally	75
Blair House Papers	104
Boeing	50
Boise	71
Browner, Carol	92
Business Week	99
Cadillac	9
California	18, 95
Los Angeles	40-41
Northridge	40
San Diego	38

Valencia	40-43
Caterpillar	14
Carlson Wagonlit Travel	54
Census, Bureau of	20
Chicago	13
Chicopee, Massachusetts	93
Christian, Doug	95-96
Citibank	21
Citicorp	56-57
Cleveland	91
Clinger-Cohen Act	48
Coast Guard	81
COBE	82-85
Colorado	
Denver	82
Commerce, Department of	49
Coopers and Lybrand	91
Customs, US	31, 86-88
Cuyahoga River	91
Defense, Department of	53-55, 74-75, 102
Distribution Region East (DDRE)	14-15
Personnel Support Center	75
Travel System	53-55
Delta Airlines	14
Denver	82
DeVillars, John	91-94
Dilbert	4, 27, 47
Disney	11, 21
Doyle, Frank	32
Draper & Kramer	90
Duke Power Company	21
Eddie Bauer	14
EDS Corp.	54, 55
Electronic Benefits Transfer (EBT)	64-67
Energy, Department of	68-69
Los Alamos	69

Sandia National Laboratories	68-69
Environmental Protection Agency (EPA)	80, 81, 91-94
Common Sense Initiative	92
StarTrack	93-94
33/50 Program	81
Export-Import Bank (Ex-Im)	16-19
Delegated Authority Program	16-19
Federal Acquistion Streamlining Act	48
Federal Aviation Administration (FAA)	61, 102
Federal Emergency Management Agency (FEMA)	13, 41
Federal Express	11
FedStats	71
First National Bank of New England	17
Florida	
Miami	86-88
Food and Drug Administration (FDA)	81, 82-85, 95-98, 102
Ford, Henry	79
Ford Motor Company	58
Forest Service	23-24
Fortune 500	47
Fuller, Warren	17-19
Gardner, Wendell	82-85
General Electric (GE)	3, 26, 31, 32, 39
Answer Center	21
General Services Administration (GSA)	31, 41, 73, 77
Auburn Paints and Chemicals Center	39-40
Gentile, Kim	56-57
Gillette	93
Goodyear	68-69
Gordon, Lynn	86-88
Green, Judson	11, 21
GTE Government Systems Corporation	77
Hadsell, David	54, 55
Hamilton, Jim	39-40
Harley Davidson	3, 28, 31
Hartley, Dan	69

Hazard Analysis and Critical Control Points (HACCP)	99
Health and Human Services, Department of	73
Hewlett-Packard	26
Home Depot	74
Hunt Valley Conference	11, 12
IBM	14, 26, 36, 37, 51-52, 54, 68
Organizational Systems Design Model	37
Idaho	71
Boise	71
Illinois	
Chicago	13
Immigration and Naturalization Service (INS)	20, 86-88
Interior, Department of	31
Internal Revenue Service (IRS)	20, 45-46, 105
International Paper	93
Jet Propulsion Laboratory (JPL)	50-52
Johnsonville Foods	11
Katzen, Sally	71
Koslow, Monique	40
Lenane, Toni	20-22
Levitt, Arthur	58-60
Liff, Stew	43
Limited	9
Livingston, Frank	90
Lockheed Martin	50-52
Los Alamos	69
Los Angeles	40-41
Maine 200 Program	81
Marine Corps	38-39
Maryland	11, 72
Hunt Valley	11
Massachusetts	91, 93
Chicopee	93
McKesson Health Systems	75
Medicare	73
MEDLINE	72

Merck	26
Miami	86-88
Miller, Loren	68-69
Minor, Milt	75
Missouri	
St. Louis	57
Motorola	3, 10, 52
NASA	50-52, 102
Pathfinder	51
National Institutes of Health (NIH)	72
National Library of Medicine	72
National Park Service	13, 23-24
Naughton, Gail	96-98
New England	91
New Jersey	17
New Mexico	
Albuquerque	68
New York	13, 36
Nordstrom	9
Northridge	40
Occupational Health and Safety Administration (OSHA)	80, 81, 88, 89-90
Asbestos Advisor	90
Office of Information and Regulatory Affairs	71
Office of Management and Budget (OMB)	64-67
Office of Personnel Management (OPM)	31
Ohio	
Cleveland	91
Outdoor Recreation Information Center (ORIC)	23-24
Pacific Telephone	73
Parker, Bill	41-42
Pathfinder	51
Paul O. Abbe, Inc.	17-19
Peck, Janice	40-43
Pennsylvania	
Philadelphia	9
Pentagon	48

Peters, Tom	11
Philadelphia	9
Postal Service	13
Privratsky, Kenneth	14-15
Radzikowski, Jack	64-67
REI	23-24
Reinvention Summit	9, 25, 28
Ritz-Carlton	9
Rocky Mountain BankCard System	49
San Diego	38
Saturn Corporation	10, 21
Scott, Donald E.	77
Seattle	23
Securities and Exchange Commission (SEC)	58-60
Selfridge, Michael	18-19
Senegal	33-35
Sheppard, John	24
Shirley, Donna	50-52
Silicon Valley Bank	18
Small Business Administration (SBA)	46, 69-71
Social Security Administration	13, 20-22, 32, 105
Southwest Airlines	10, 25
Spalding Sports Worldwide	93-94
Spiegel	14
Sprint	73
St. Louis	57
StarTrack	93-94
Stayer, Ralph	11
Summit Conference on Reinventing Government	9, 25, 28
Sweetman, William	93-94
Texas Instruments	93
Thermo Electron	25
Thompson, Joe	36-38
Treasury, Department of	49
US Business Advisor	69-71
USAA Insurance	21

Valencia	40-43
Veterans Affairs, Department of (VA)	36-38, 40-43, 74-75
Virginia	72
Visa	9, 49
Wal-Mart	14-15, 25
Walt Disney Attractions	11, 21
Washington	
Seattle	23
Washington, DC	13, 96, 104
Weather Service	102
White House Conference on Small Business	70
Williams, Anne	33-35
Xerox	11

To order additional copies of **Businesslike Government: Lessons Learned From America's Best Companies** at $8 per copy:

- use the handy order form below
- e-mail your Visa, MasterCard, or Discover/NOVUS credit card orders to *orders@gpo.gov*
- fax your credit card orders to (202) 512-2250
- phone your credit card orders to (202) 512-1800

You can also order from any of the 24 nationwide *U.S. Government Bookstores*—check the yellow or blue pages of your phone book for a store near you, or check the U.S. Government Printing Office web site at:

http://www.access.gpo.gov/su_docs/sale/abkst001.html

Note: Purchasers of 100 or more copies sent to a single address will receive a 25 percent discount.

United States Government INFORMATION

Order Processing Code: * 8131

Charge your order. It's easy!

VISA MasterCard DISCOVER/NOVUS

Fax your order: (202) 512-2250
Phone your order: (202) 512-1800

Qty.	Stock Number	Title	Price Each	Total Price
	040-000-00695-8	Businesslike Government: Lessons Learned From America's Best Companies	$8.00	

Price includes regular shipping and handling and is subject to change.
International customers please add 25 percent.

Total Order

Check method of payment:
❑ Check payable to Superintendent of Documents
❑ GPO Deposit Account ☐☐☐☐☐☐☐–☐
❑ VISA ❑ MasterCard ❑ Discover/NOVUS
☐☐☐☐ ☐☐☐☐ ☐☐☐☐ ☐☐☐☐
☐☐☐☐ (expiration date) *Thank you for your order!*

Personal name (Please type or print)

Company name

Street address

City, State, Zip code

Daytime phone including area code

Authorizing signature

10/97

**Mail to: Superintendent of Documents, PO Box 371954
Pittsburgh, PA 15250-7954**

ISBN 0-16-049288-2

90000